the BOYS team

amy schwartz

the BOYS team

a richard jackson book
atheneum books for young readers
new york london toronto sydney singapore

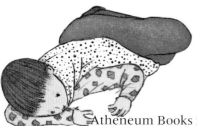

Atheneum Books for Young Readers
An imprint of Simon & Schuster Children's Publishing Division
1230 Avenue of the Americas
New York, New York 10020

Book design by Michael Nelson
The text of this book is set in Meridien.
The illustrations are rendered in watercolor and pen & ink.

Printed in Hong Kong
2 4 6 8 10 9 7 5 3 1

Library of Congress Cataloging-in-Publication Data
Schwartz, Amy.
The Boys Team / by Amy Schwartz.—1st ed.
p.   cm.
"A Richard Jackson book."
Summary: A five-year-old boy talks about what he and
his two friends do during their week at kindergarten.
ISBN 0-689-84138-8
[1. Nursey schools—Fiction. 2. Schools—Fiction.] I. Title.
PZ7.S406 Bo 2001
[E]—dc21   00-037126

FIRST
EDITION

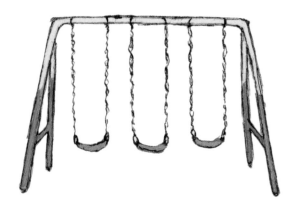

for Julie Lipton

We're the Boys Team,
We three.
Oscar,
Eddie
And me.

We chase Julia C.

We also chase Julia D.

And sometimes, Sophie P.

Oscar is the boss,
But not of me!

We're bigger
Than the Four-Fives!
We're bigger
Than the Three-Day Threes!
We're bigger
Than the Two-Day Twos!

Kindergartners
Rule
The School!

We three
Are Mighty Ducks.
We build with LEGOS.
We build with blocks.

We eat pizza
For our lunch.
Apple juice,
And Cap'n Crunch.

We love lunch!
We hate nap!
We never sleep!
We never fight!

Well, sometimes we do.
At music
Eddie jabbed me in the chest.
I bit his hand.
Sophie told.
We were benched.

We're the same size,
Oscar,
Eddie
And me.

Except I'm taller
Than Oscar.
And Eddie.
Because of my curls.

At meeting
Ms. Brown
Asked us
To name our pets.

I said
I had
39 goldfish
And a parrot.

Actually,
I don't have any pets.
But,
If I did have any pets,
I would have
39 goldfish
And a parrot.

On Monday the Boys Team
Has Karate.
And on Tuesday,
Swim.
Wednesday,
Eddie comes home with me.
Thursday I go home with him.

Friday,
We play all three,
Oscar,
Eddie
And me.

Unless I have plans
With Julia D.
Once she
Chased me
With Tiffany.

I pulled Tiffany's hair!
I threw Tiffany down the stairs!
Julia D. screamed real loud.
After our time-out . . .

We ate cookies
And clementines.
We stirred sugar
In our tea.
I laughed
With Julia D.

At Fortune House
Sophie P.
Blew a kiss
That landed on me.
We crawled under tables,
We counted the fish.
We ordered six dumplings.
I ate three.

On Halloween
I was Darth Vader.
Oscar was
Darth Vader.
Eddie was
Darth Vader.

We trick-or-treated
Up the street
And down the street.
Up the street
And down.

I trick-or-treated
140 pieces of candy.
It was
The best day
Of my life.

At Christmas
Oscar got
New ice skates.
And a hockey stick.
And a puck.
"*And* I'm going skiing!"
He said.
"For five days!"

That's when
I mentioned
Head gliding.
"It's where
You put skis
On your head.
Then,
You stand on your head.
And ski,"
I told Oscar.

"That's what
I'm doing
For vacation."

We're the Boys Team,
We three!
We're as good friends
As friends can be,
Oscar,
Eddie
And me.

Boys only!
That's what we say.

Except on Tuesday,
We let in Sophie P.
And on Wednesday,
Julia C.
And on Thursday, even
Julia D.

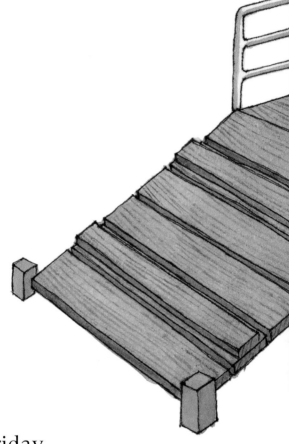

But on Friday,
Every Friday,
We are only three,
Oscar,
Eddie
And me.
We are Mutant Sharks!
We take over the park!

We build a fort,
It's just for us.
Because—
We're the Boys Team,
We three.
Oscar,
Eddie

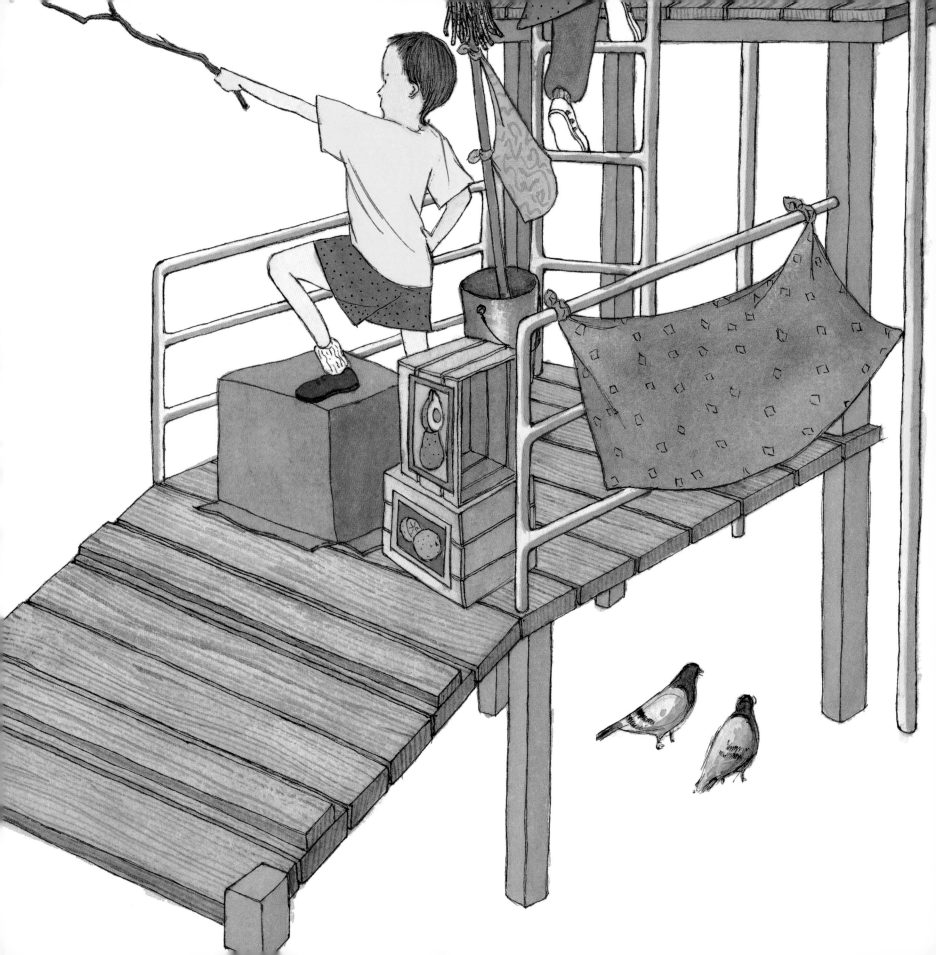

And me—

Jacob!